19

Animals with Jobs

Navy Dolphins

Judith Janda Presnall

KidHaven Press, an imprint of Gale Group, Inc.

10911 Technology Place, San Diego, CA 92127

Dedication

For my husband, Lance, who shares in my book project travels.

Acknowledgments

The author wishes to thank Tom LaPuzza, public affairs officer at the Space and Naval Warfare Systems Center, San Diego, for helpful comments and suggestions, for answering many questions, and for searching for photographs to include in this book. Dr. Sam Ridgway, senior medical officer for the Marine Mammal Program and the U.S. Navy's first dolphin veterinarian for comments and suggestions. His book, *The Dolphin Doctor*, was helpful on this project.

Library of Congress Cataloging-in-Publication Data
Presnall, Judith Janda.
    Navy Dolphins / By Judith Janda Presnall.
       p. cm. — (Animals with jobs)
    Includes bibliographical references and index.
    Summary: Discusses the U.S. Navy's use of dolphins including dolphin behavior and training, tasks learned, participation in world conflicts, and the Navy's Marine Mammal Program.
    ISBN 0–7377–0675–9 (hardback alk. paper)
    1. Bottlenose dolphin—War use—Juvenile literature. 2. United States. Navy—History—20th century—Juvenile literature. [1. Bottlenose dolphin—War use. 2. Dolphins—War use. 3. United States. Navy.] I. Title. II. Series.
    UH100.5.B68 P74 2002
    359.4'24—dc21
2001001441

Contents

Introduction
Unusual U.S. Navy Recruits 4

Chapter One
The Amazing Navy Dolphin 8

Chapter Two
Studying the Dolphin 15

Chapter Three
Training Dolphins for Military Tasks 22

Chapter Four
Other Projects 30

Notes 39

Glossary 40

Organizations to Contact 42

For Further Exploration 44

Index 45

Picture Credits 47

About the Author 48

Introduction

Unusual U.S. Navy Recruits

The U. S. Navy began a Marine Mammal Program in 1960 to take advantage of the dolphin's natural capabilities: **sonar**, underwater hearing, and deep diving. Sonar, also called **echolocating**, is the way a dolphin sends and receives messages. The dolphin's special sonar enables it to perform many tasks that humans cannot. A dolphin can find an enemy swimming in the water at night, for example. A dolphin can also find bombs planted near ships or under piers. Their superior hearing allows them to respond to clicks and other sounds when they are in training for tasks such as rescuing lost divers and dropped equipment. They can dive deeper (one thousand feet) and swim faster (twenty-five miles per hour) than humans. All of these unique abilities make dolphins valuable to the Navy.

Marine Mammal Program

The Navy's Marine Mammal Program and training center is located on Point Loma in San Diego, California.

A dolphin responds to a trainer's command.

In more than forty years, the U.S. Navy has trained over two hundred dolphins.

A dolphin serves for up to thirty years, and costs the Navy $15,000 to $20,000 a year for food and medication. Today's navy dolphins live in open-mesh pens in the bays and harbors of the Pacific Ocean. In addition, since many pens are grouped together, the dolphins can communicate with one another.

Of the estimated sixty-five dolphins at Point Loma, about half serve in three special units in the Navy's Marine Mammal Systems. Each unit of dolphins spe-

The U.S. Navy favors dolphins for many underwater jobs.

The Point Loma training center houses navy dolphins in open-mesh pens.

cializes either in detecting floating mines, finding buried mines, or detecting and marking locations of swimmers. The Navy can quickly transfer these dolphins by military planes to any part of the world. The other half makes up three groups: some dolphins are retired and no longer in service. The others are involved in training and research.

Chapter One

The Amazing Navy Dolphin

The bottlenose dolphins that work for the U.S. Navy are trained to save the lives of sailors and marines during wartime. To accomplish this, handlers train the dolphins to detect swimmers and underwater mines.

Bottlenose Dolphins Are Preferred

Although more than thirty species of dolphins exist, not all species are used in the U.S. Navy's work. The Navy prefers using bottlenose dolphins for a number of reasons. Bottlenose dolphins populate a wide variety of the world's oceans, so they can be used in many places. They are reliable and friendly. And their size allows them to be carried easily in boats, helicopters, and airplanes.

Dolphins in Wars

Bottlenose dolphins were first used in the military during the Vietnam War. The Navy sent five dolphins to Cam Ranh Bay for a fifteen-month period. The dolphins

The U.S. Navy prefers bottlenose dolphins because they are reliable, friendly, and fast learners.

Bottlenose dolphins were first used in a swimmer defense program during the Vietnam War.

patrolled the dock areas in the harbor as well as the U.S. ships anchored there.

The Navy called this effort the swimmer defense program. The dolphins "spot and tag" enemy swimmers sent to blow up the ammunition pier or to plant explosives beneath American ships. "If someone was in the water at night," a former employee says, "you could be sure he wasn't friendly."[1] Because of the constant threat of such a possibility, the dolphins were on duty every night.

Finding an Enemy Swimmer

A dolphin prowls slowly around **moored** vessels, searching the area using its sonar. It carries a marker device on its nose. If the dolphin locates a diver, it bumps the person causing the marker to release.

The marker has a flashing **strobe light** and marks the diver's location in the dark waters. The dolphin then races to its handler's boat, jumps in, and the boat speeds from the area. Meanwhile, armed security patrols move in on the flashing strobe light and capture the diver.

Dolphins in the Persian Gulf

The next combat duty that engaged dolphins was the Iraqi invasion of Kuwait. The United States had sent a fleet of warships to the Persian Gulf to protect oil shipments. During an eight-month period in 1987 and 1988, the Navy stationed a team of five bottlenose dolphins and twenty-five men in that area. As in Vietnam, the dolphins patrolled the harbor in Bahrain, protecting anchored ships from enemy swimmers who may have tried to plant explosives. The dolphins guarded the **perimeter** of the USS *La Salle* flagship, a huge floating base housing more than four hundred American sailors.

Dolphins Locate Mines Using Sonar

The Navy also trains dolphins to detect undersea explosives, called **sea mines**. Made of metal or plastic, sea mines are **complex** bombs that blow up ships. These sea mines contain computers with sensors that can detect a mass of metal like a ship, the noise of a ship, or the waves a ship makes.

Handlers train dolphins to know the difference between the mines and the natural environment of rocks, coral, and shellfish. When a dolphin goes sea mine hunting with its handler, it jumps from its pen to a padded mat on a smaller boat and rides to the mine areas. Once there, the dolphin slips into the water and its handler moves into an inflatable boat that is less likely to trigger a mine explosion.

Dolphins were used to guard the USS La Salle *(front, right) and other ships during the Persian Gulf War.*

A trained dolphin knows the difference between a coral reef (pictured) and a mine.

Marking a Sea Mine

With his nose, the dolphin tows a package that contains three attached pieces: the marker/anchor, the line, and a float. When the dolphin finds a sea mine, it marks the mass by dropping the package near the mine. The package then splits apart.

The anchor stays on the bottom, marking the location of the mine. The float drifts to the surface. In between is the line. Human divers see the float and follow the attached line to the marker and take the mine apart.

Sometimes mines are moored, or floating, thirty to fifty feet from the sea bottom on a long cable. The mine, often in very deep water, is at the top of the cable and an anchoring device is on the sea bottom. In this situation, the dolphin attaches the marker to the cable below the mine case. Sometimes the marker contains an explosive device that blows up the mine once the dolphin has returned to its boat and has been whisked away.

Recent Dolphin Duties

Dolphins also perform protection jobs outside of military situations. For example, U.S. Navy dolphins patrolled the coast of California during the 1996 Republican Convention in San Diego.

Studying the Dolphin

The Navy had to learn a lot about dolphins before it could train them for active duty. By studying dolphins, the Navy hoped to improve sonar technology as well as the design of their ships, submarines, and torpedoes. The Navy performed a variety of sonar experiments with dolphins and examined their hearing, speed swimming, and breathing.

Sonar Ability

The primary asset of the dolphin is its sonar, or echolocation, ability. While swimming, the dolphin sends out a series of clicks from its bulging forehead. The clicks race through the water until they bump into something solid. It could be a fish, a reef, or an enemy, such as a shark. An echo then bounces back to the dolphin and creates an image in its brain.

Sonar gives information such as size, shape, and distance of various objects. By swinging its head from

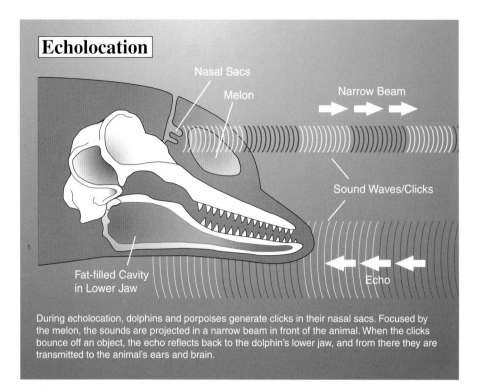

Echolocation

Nasal Sacs

Melon

Narrow Beam

Sound Waves/Clicks

Fat-filled Cavity
in Lower Jaw

Echo

During echolocation, dolphins and porpoises generate clicks in their nasal sacs. Focused by the melon, the sounds are projected in a narrow beam in front of the animal. When the clicks bounce off an object, the echo reflects back to the dolphin's lower jaw, and from there they are transmitted to the animal's ears and brain.

side to side, the dolphin can cover an even wider target area. Whether day or night, or in cloudy water, dolphins can echolocate, or sense, a softball-size object as far away as three hundred feet—the length of a football field.

Sonar Experiments in 1960

At California's Marineland of the Pacific, scientists working for the Office of Naval Research studied a dolphin named Zippy. Dr. Kenneth Norris, curator of Marineland, explained the process of teaching Zippy to first accept human touching. "We wouldn't give her anything to eat unless she let us touch her. She was fed from the rim of the tank, and our first big job was to get her to stay still while one of us cupped our hands over her eyes. She didn't like that at all, but she got used to it."[2]

The purpose of the experiment was to make sure that Zippy could not see the objects upon which she was echolocating. Therefore, Zippy's eyes had to be covered. The scientists used gloves on their hands to cover Zippy's eyes. And finally, they covered Zippy's eyes with rubber suction cups. It took four months of daily training sessions for Zippy to adjust to wearing soft rubber suction cups over her eyes for the sonar experiments.

The scientists then shifted a target (a large button at the end of a slender rod) to various locations throughout Zippy's thirty-five-foot diameter tank. Even as the scientists reduced the target size (down to one inch in diameter), Zippy was able to locate it without trouble.

Another sonar test included covering Zippy's pinpoint ear canals to prove that dolphins do not need ears to **maneuver**. In a third test, the scientists demonstrated that the dolphin's sonar travels in a straight beam coming from the forehead.

Current Sonar Experiments

One experiment seemed to prove that a dolphin's sonar may be better than its vision. A handler put an object in a black plastic box underwater. The dolphin echolocated through the box on the object and then had to match the object to an identical one held by someone out of the water. (Since sonar does not work out of water, the dolphin was now using its eyes.) It swam to the person holding the matching object. The dolphin was successful in matching thirteen out of sixteen objects.

Breathing Technique Aids in Diving Tasks

Dolphins are mammals that must take oxygen from the air. Dolphins and their relatives—the whales and porpoises—must surface to breathe through the **blow-**

To conduct sonar experiments, scientists cover dolphins' eyes.

Dolphins identify objects out of the water using their eyes instead of sonar.

holes on the tops of their heads. When they pop out of the water, they puff out used air and suck in fresh air. Before it dips under the waves, a dolphin's blowhole snaps shut to keep water out.

Dolphins normally catch a breath of air two or three times each minute. But on dives, they may stay down four to six minutes before they surface. Dolphins' lungs can handle underwater changes in pressure, which allows them to dive deeply and perform tasks—such as finding lost equipment and divers.

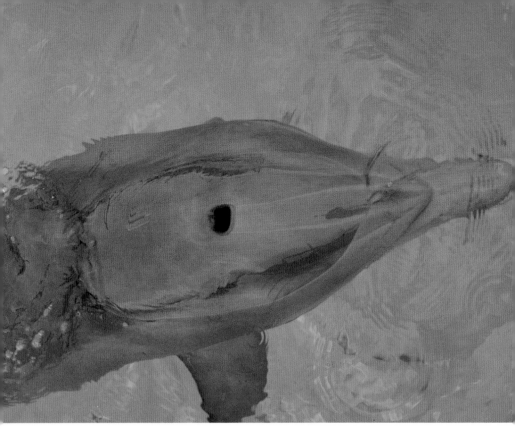

Dolphins breathe through the blowholes on top of their heads.

A One Thousand-Foot Dive

In the 1960s, the Navy tested the diving ability of dolphins by using an automobile steering wheel with a buzzer in the center of the steering wheel. Handlers attached a measured electrical cable to the steering wheel and lowered it into the water. Trained to respond to the buzzer, the dolphin tilted the **submerged** wheel, an action which turned off the buzzer. When the buzzing stopped, the researchers in the boat knew that the dolphin had reached the target. The deepest diving depth was one thousand feet.

This exercise proved that dolphins could make repeated dives without experiencing "the bends," or decompression sickness, as do human divers. In later experiments dolphins brought tools and supplies to **aquanauts**, or marine scientists, and located lost equipment. Dolphins are easy to train because they learn fast and respond quickly to humans.

Training Dolphins for Military Tasks

Dolphins must train almost everyday. The tasks that dolphins learn are called behaviors. Some can learn twenty or more behaviors. Individual dolphins do not learn at the same speed, or even learn the same behaviors. If a dolphin is exceptionally good at one task, trainers will expand on that behavior. Experienced dolphins may work with several different trainers.

Training Takes Patience and Trust

Trainers of any animal must first gain its trust. For example, to get a dolphin to leave the water—whether for weigh-in or going into a boat—the animal must have complete trust in its trainer. For a marine animal, being beached means death. Thus, training a dolphin to leave the water must be done a little at a time. For example, to get a dolphin to slide out of the water onto a mat,

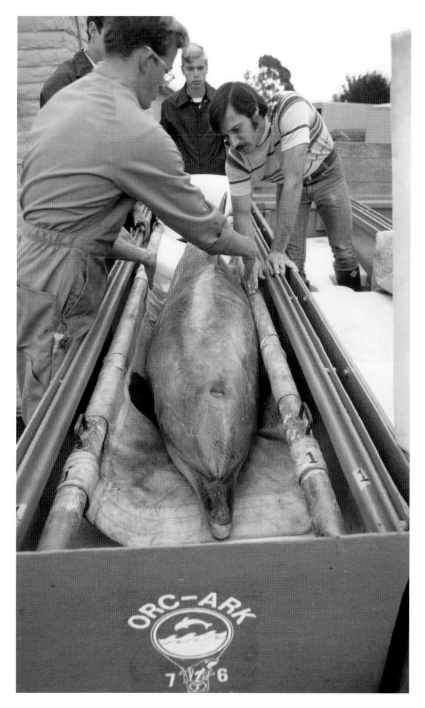

A dolphin is prepared for transport.

A trainer builds trust by hand-feeding a dolphin.

a trainer starts with just the dolphin's nose. Next, the dolphin slides its head onto the mat. The dolphin will progress to sliding out more of its body each time. This must be done daily for weeks, before the task is learned.

First Dolphin Trainee: Tuffy

Usually dolphins need to be tamed before they can be trained. One dolphin, named Tuffy, was in poor health when transferred from Pacific Ocean Park in Santa Monica, California, to the Point Mugu Naval Base where early dolphin training took place. Tuffy was feisty and difficult to handle and had skin sores from clashes with other dolphins.

Trainer Debbie started her first day of taming Tuffy by feeding him fish from the outside edge of his pool. After the first day, Debbie worked inside the waist-deep pool, wearing a rubber wetsuit. Soon Tuffy accepted her touching his jaw and back fin.

Taming Leads to Retrieving

As taming continued, Debbie began **retrieving** lessons. With much coaxing, Tuffy learned that if he did something for Debbie, he would be rewarded with a fish. Tuffy mastered the skill of "finding and bringing back" an object quickly.

Debbie's notes reveal her happiness at Tuffy's progress: "EUREKA! A.M. Fed 11 lb.—worked well— spent most of my time working with [Tuffy] staying still while being touched. Retrieved well and instantly. Stayed still longer and didn't seem as touchy."[3]

One day a zipper on Debbie's wetsuit got caught behind Tuffy's flipper. Instantly, the dolphin whirled around and bit her hand, leaving eleven bleeding puncture holes in her palm and wrist. "It was strange," Debbie said. "After that bite Tuffy seemed to trust me completely. I could touch him anywhere, I could rub him, and I could pull on any part of his body. He became more willing to work."[4]

Hand and Noise Signals

For the most part, trainers use arm and hand signals as commands. Their goal is to instruct the dolphin to associate a different arm/hand signal with a different behavior. Sounds such as whistles, toy metal crickets, bells, and even strobe lights that click with each flash are used to start or end a task. For example, to call a dolphin back to the boat, the trainer lowers a flashing/clicking strobe light into the water and the animal responds by swimming to the boat.

U.S. Navy researchers set one primary training goal for their dolphins: to use them untethered, or unleashed, in the open seas for research or military tasks. It takes about six months of constant, steadfast training before a dolphin is considered trustworthy and sufficiently trained for open-sea tasks.

Open-Sea Training

Open-sea training is done directly in ocean pens. Using fish for rewards, trainers begin with pinger, or noise, recall so the dolphin comes when called. The dolphins are grouped together in the pen for socialization, and then separated for training. Sometimes for a training session, handlers place an experienced dolphin in the same training pen because the trainees imitate the trained dolphin and learn more quickly. Some dolphins

Trainers use arm and hand signals to communicate with dolphins.

who are trained in the open sea will be used to detect mines.

Hunting for Mines

Training dolphins to use their sonar to locate and mark submerged sea mines is accomplished at a slow pace. The Navy began this type of training in 1975. To train for finding real mines, dolphins first practice looking for fake mines with no explosives.

Handlers train a dolphin to swim closer and closer to a target mine, but never to touch it. First, a minelike shape—oval, sphere, or square—perhaps four feet in size, is placed near the swimming dolphin. Whenever the dolphin swims close to the object, the trainer blows his whistle, and then rewards the dolphin with a fish. Soon the dolphin realizes that whenever it swims close to this object, it is rewarded. Thus, it tends to swim close to it often.

If the dolphin touches or swims too close to the object, it is not rewarded. Eventually the dolphin is given a marker and learns to place it near the object,

An exploding mine can hurt or kill a dolphin just as it would a human.

but not on it—again being rewarded for remaining a safe distance from the mine. This training takes four or five years before the dolphin is ready to **deploy** with an operations unit.

Mine Hunting Technology in 2000

The U.S. Navy tested its newest advance in military technology employing dolphins in Alaska in 2000. The Navy built an experimental version of a fighter bass boat, called an EX-8 Low Visible Craft. Two navy personnel ride in the boat. In the front seat, a dolphin handler gives out fish treats after the animal places radio markers near mines. A navy **SEAL specialist** in the back seat maps the radio marker devices on his laptop computer screen. Later, human divers use the digital map to find the tagged mines and attach remote controlled explosives to them. The mines are set off as the boats make their way to the beach.

Thus, navy dolphins help humans in dangerous tasks, and, in some cases, can perform better than humans.

Chapter Four

Other Projects

The Navy demands a high degree of performance on the part of dolphins. Each dolphin trainee learns a given task and practices it until it is accomplished the same way each time.

First Success: SeaLab II

The Navy's first success in assisting divers under water involved the dolphin Tuffy. In September 1965, Tuffy received national attention for his work on the U.S. Navy experiment SeaLab II in the waters off La Jolla, California.

To prepare for the underwater laboratory tasks, Tuffy trained for six weeks. He learned to respond to a noise buzzer for the tests. Then the dolphin, his trainers, and researchers flew by helicopter to Mission Bay. Tuffy was then loaded onto a boat that took him to a temporary holding pen in the open ocean near the SeaLab II.

Dolphins must train for many weeks to be ready to assist divers in underwater tasks.

Making Deliveries

The primary purpose of the SeaLab II experiment was to ensure that dolphins could be trained to work untethered in the open sea and be trusted not to swim away. These tasks took place in murky waters where humans could neither see well nor make repeated dives.

The SeaLab II was a one hundred ton, fifty-seven-foot long white metal canister "house" located two hun-

Tuffy the dolphin and navy divers work outside SeaLab II.

dred feet below the water surface. It hung by cables and hoses attached to the floating *Berkone* "Mothership." The *Berkone* was the headquarters from which navy personnel directed all the operations. Three different teams of ten aquanauts lived in the SeaLab II for two-week periods. Tuffy brought tools, mail, soft drinks, and even his own packed-fish rewards to the aquanauts.

Practicing to Rescue Lost Divers

The water at two hundred feet was shadowy, making it impossible for aquanauts to see very far. One of Tuffy's jobs in the test was to rescue lost aquanauts. Using a noise buzzer, one aquanaut buzzed Tuffy to come down to the SeaLab II habitat. This aquanaut placed a ring on Tuffy's nose with a line attached and shut off his buzzer.

About one hundred eighty feet away, a second aquanaut pretended to be lost. He signaled Tuffy with his buzzer to bring the line. Tuffy brought the line to the lost diver, who removed it from Tuffy's nose and followed the line back home.

Later, equipment was updated to a spring-loaded winding spool on a stand. The dolphin responded to the buzzing call by taking a line from the rescue reel to the "lost" diver. The diver was then "pulled" back to the SeaLab II habitat.

Recovering Lost Equipment

Handlers also trained dolphins to recover lost equipment. Using dolphins for the retrieval of expensive equipment has saved the Navy thousands of dollars.

Dolphins learn to retrieve missiles that fall into the ocean after being fired from ships.

Many devices—often with complex computer guidance systems—used in ocean **missile** tests are costly and valuable. This high-priced equipment drops into the sea after being fired from airplanes, submarines, or surface ships. Consequently, the Navy tries to recover the pieces after they fall into the ocean.

When the Navy used human divers to retrieve weapons, it was expensive. It took two divers to retrieve the missile, and two other divers, halfway down, to keep an eye on the first pair. Also, on the surface, the Navy had to provide medical personnel and equipment for divers who might experience difficulty. Humans, using scuba gear, can dive down to only about 130 feet. But dolphins can easily dive to depths between 690 and 990 feet to retrieve equipment.

Dolphins' Eyes and Ears Help Locate Valuables

When using a dolphin to retrieve, navy personnel attached a sound-emitting beacon to the detachable

A dolphin swims easily in shallow or deep water.

cradle on the missile. As soon as the cradle hit the water, it began transmitting noises.

A dolphin **homed** in on the target immediately. The dolphin could hear the clicking noise from a distance and would see the flashing light when it swam closer. The dolphin then marked the location by dropping a "separating" package which it carried on its snout. The package contained an anchor, reel of line, and an ascending buoy, which marked the sunken cradle for divers.

Open Ocean Training Problems

Although dolphins can do more than humans underwater, their unpredictable nature makes them difficult to use. Trainer Don McSheehy discussed several problems the Navy had with dolphins in open ocean advanced training. One is boat following. Some dolphins begin to follow a different boat, thus losing track of their task.

In addition, since food is used as a reward, dolphins refuse to work once they can feed on other fish in the ocean. The dolphin will just leave and not perform tasks for the trainers' fish rewards.

Dolphins also can become scared. They may see something—maybe a shark or whales, which they are unaccustomed to in their pens. Either they bolt for home, or they will quit working on the spot.

Dolphins will also become distracted and leave to surf or **bow** ride. One dolphin loved to surf so much that she would leave and go to the local surfing spot to surf right along with the human surfers.

Dolphins can be easily distracted in the open ocean.

Sometimes weather causes trouble. It must be calm to perform experiments. Unpredictable rough seas may cause the trainer to lose visual contact with the dolphin. When that happens, the dolphin has only the boat's engine as a homing device. It may leave and appear back home in its pen within twenty-four hours.

Budget Cuts Reduce Training Programs

In 1991, Congress reduced the Navy's Marine Mammal Program budget. This forced the Navy to close down their training centers in Hawaii and Key West, Florida, and eventually move the dolphins to the Point Loma, California facility. These unusual navy recruits have proven to be very useful in helping the navy and will continue to be helpful in the future.

Notes

Chapter One: The Amazing Navy Dolphin

1. John May, ed., *The Greenpeace Book of Dolphins*. New York: Sterling Publishing Co., 1990, p. 125.

Chapter Two: Studying the Dolphin

2. Wesley S. Griswold, "The Case of the Blindfolded Dolphin," *Popular Science*, August 1960, p. 184.

Chapter Three: Training Dolphins for Military Tasks

3. Sam Ridgway, *The Dolphin Doctor*. Dublin, NH: Yankee Publishing Inc., 1987, p. 65.
4. Ridgway, *The Dolphin Doctor*, p. 65.

Glossary

aquanaut: an underwater researcher or scientist

blowhole: An opening on the top of a dolphin's head used for breathing and also for sound production.

bow: the front section of a ship or boat

complex: intricate or containing many complicated elements

deploy: to move forces of a military unit to a certain area

echolocate: A means of finding objects by sending out sounds and receiving the echoes that bounce back from the object.

homing: to be guided to a place or target by sensing signals

maneuver: physical movement that requires skill

missile: a weapon that is propelled at a target

moor: fastened with an anchor

perimeter: the outer boundary of an area

retrieve: to bring back; to find and carry back

SEAL Specialist: SEAL stands for Sea-Air-Land, highly trained forces who perform dangerous missions.

sea mine: An explosive apparatus placed on the ocean bottom or suspended in the ocean meant to destroy ships and sailors without being easily set off by ocean currents or sea animals.

sonar: A device for finding things in water either by the reflection of sound waves or by echolocation.

strobe light: A flickering lamp that produces very short, intense flashes of light, along with a clicking noise.

submerge: to place under water

Organizations to Contact

Dolphin Research Center
P.O. Box 522875
Marathon Shores, FL 33052
(305) 289-1121
www.dolphins.org

This education and research facility houses a family of Atlantic bottlenose dolphins and California sea lions. The website offers information on dolphins living at the facility, adopting a dolphin, and getting questions answered.

Sea World of California
Education Department
500 Sea World Drive
San Diego, CA 92109–7995
(619) 226-3834
www.seaworld.org/bottlenose

This site lists fourteen categories in their table of contents, such as physical characteristics, behavior, diet and eating habits, and communication and echolocation.

U.S. Navy Marine Mammal History Page
Attn: Tom LaPuzza, SSC San Diego Public Affairs Officer

53560 Hull Street
San Diego, CA 92152-5001
(619) 553-2724
www.spawar.navy.mil

Beginning in 1960, the Navy became interested in the dolphin. This site discusses the history, its programs, and also its uses of sea lions and whales.

For Further Exploration

June Behrens, *Dolphins!* Chicago: Children's Press, 1989. Using colored photos, this book describes and illustrates the appearance, reproduction, social behavior, and intelligence of the remarkable dolphin.

Janelle Hatherly and Delia Nicholls, *Dolphins and Porpoises.* New York: Facts on File, 1990. Through many color photos, this book relates the physical characteristics, habits, and natural environment of dolphins and porpoises.

Elizabeth Simpson Smith, *A Dolphin Goes to School— The Story of Squirt, a Trained Dolphin.* New York: Morrow and Co., 1986. This is the true story of one bottlenose dolphin that was captured and trained and eventually appeared in marine shows all across the country.

Index

aquanaut rescue, 33

behaviors, 22
"bends, the," 21
Berkone, 32
blowholes, 18–19
bombs, 11–14, 27–29
bottlenose dolphins, 8
bow riding, 36
breaching, 22, 24
breathing, 18–19

Debbie, 25–26
dives
    depth of, 4, 20, 35
    time under water, 19
duties
    locating mines, 11–14
    patrolling coasts, 14
    swimmer defense
        program, 8, 10–11

echolocation
    experiments using,
        16–18

information from,
    15–16
uses of, 4
EX-8 Low Visible Craft, 29

forehead
    clicks from, 15
    sonar and, 17

hearing, sense of, 4

Marineland of the Pacific,
    16–18
Marine Mammal Pro-
    gram, 4–7, 37–38
McSheehy, Don, 36
mines, 11–14, 27–29
missile recovery, 33–36
Mothership, 32

Navy SEAL specialist, 29
Norris, Kenneth, 16

Pacific Ocean Park, 25
Persian Gulf, 11

Point Loma, 4, 38
Point Mugu Naval Base, 25

retrieving, 25

SeaLab II, 30, 32–33
SEAL specialist, 29
sea mines, 11–14, 27–29
sight, sense of, 17
signals, 26, 30, 35
sonar
  experiments using,
    16–18
  forehead and, 17
  information from,
    15–16
  uses of, 4
strobe lights, 11
surfing, 36
swimmer defense
  program, 8, 10–11
swimming speed, 4

taming, 25
training
  breaching, 22, 24
  imitation, 26
  to locate mines, 27–29
  in open sea, 26–27, 36
  patience needed, 24, 26,
    29
  problems with, 36–37
  signals used in, 26, 30
  taming, 25
  trust in trainer and,
    22
Tuffy, 25–26, 30, 33

USS *La Salle* (ship), 11

Vietnam War, 8, 10

weather, 36–37

Zippy, 16–17

Picture Credits

About the Author

Award-winning author Judith Janda Presnall writes nonfiction books for children and young adults. Some of her books include *Oprah Winfrey, Rachel Carson, The Giant Panda, Mount Rushmore, Artificial Organs,* and *Life on Alcatraz.* In addition to *Navy Dolphins,* Presnall has also written *Horse Therapists, Police Dogs, Animal Actors,* and *Guide Dogs* for Kidhaven Press's Animals with Jobs series.

Presnall graduated from the University of Wisconsin, Whitewater. After teaching business classes, she changed careers and now writes full-time. In 1997, the California Writers Club honored Presnall with the Jack London Award for meritorious service. She and her husband Lance live in Los Angeles, California, with their three cats. They have two adult children, Kaye and Kory.